JACKIE ROBINSON
BREAKS THE
COLOR BARRIER

by Bo Smolka

Greatest Events in
SPORTS HISTORY

SportsZone

An Imprint of Abdo Publishing
www.abdopublishing.com

www.abdopublishing.com

Published by Abdo Publishing, a division of ABDO, PO Box 398166, Minneapolis, Minnesota 55439. Copyright © 2015 by Abdo Consulting Group, Inc. International copyrights reserved in all countries. No part of this book may be reproduced in any form without written permission from the publisher. SportsZone™ is a trademark and logo of Abdo Publishing.

Printed in the United States of America, North Mankato, Minnesota
092014
012015

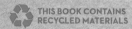
THIS BOOK CONTAINS
RECYCLED MATERIALS

Cover Photo: John Rooney/AP Images
Interior Photos: John Rooney/AP Images, 1; AP Images, 4, 9, 10, 13, 14, 17, 23, 29; Bettmann/Corbis, 7, 24, 27, 30, 33, 34, 36, 38, 41; Ed Widdis/AP Images, 18; Nam Y. Huh/AP Images, 43

Editor: Chrös McDougall
Series Designer: Craig Hinton

Library of Congress Control Number: 2014944196

Cataloging-in-Publication Data
Smolka, Bo.
 Jackie Robinson breaks the color barrier / Bo Smolka.
  p. cm. -- (Greatest events in sports history)
ISBN 978-1-62403-594-4 (lib. bdg.)
Includes bibliographical references and index.
1. Baseball--United States--History--Juvenile literature. 2. African American baseball players--United States--Juvenile literature.   I. Title.
796.357--dc23

2014944196

CONTENTS

CHAPTER 1

Baseball's Color Barrier

T he Newark Little Giants took the field for an exhibition game in 1887 against the Chicago White Stockings. Set to start for the Giants was George Stovey, a black pitcher. White Stockings player-manager Adrian "Cap" Anson reacted angrily.

"What's he doing here?" Anson implied. "Get him off the field!" Anson said his team would not play against any team with black players.

Scenes such as those were common at that time. The United States was not very united at all. It was deeply divided by race. In many places, particularly in the South, blacks faced discrimination of every kind. Signs outside hotels, restaurants,

MOSES FLEETWOOD WALKER

On May 1, 1884, Moses Fleetwood Walker played catcher for Toledo, Ohio, in the major league American Association. He is widely credited with being the first black major leaguer. A few black players followed him. However, baseball's color line was drawn soon after. By the late 1800s, there were no blacks in organized baseball.

theaters, and pools read: "Whites only." That same discrimination extended to baseball.

By 1900, black players were not allowed in organized baseball. That included major league teams and the minor league teams associated with them. No official rule prohibited black players. But team owners would not hire them. This became known as baseball's color barrier, or color line.

With organized baseball off-limits, top black players joined all-black teams. These teams played in what came to be known as the Negro Leagues. Most white fans paid no attention to the Negro Leagues. But by the 1940s, that began to change. Sometimes, Negro Leagues teams played offseason exhibition games against major leaguers. The Negro Leagues teams often won. In some cities, Negro Leagues teams rented major league stadiums and played there. White reporters took notice of their skills. They began to write about how good the best Negro Leagues players were.

Members of the Negro Leagues' Chicago Giants look out of the dugout in 1942.

But Major League Baseball (MLB) refused to open its doors to black players. MLB's commissioner, Judge Kenesaw Mountain Landis, was strongly opposed to black players in the major leagues. He showed this belief when the Pittsburgh Pirates tried to sign catcher Josh Gibson. Gibson was a star in the Negro Leagues. He wowed fans with towering home runs. Many people compared him with Babe Ruth. In 1943, the Pirates wanted to sign Gibson. But Landis would not allow it.

"The colored ballplayers have their own league," Landis said. "Let them stay in their own league."

Black sportswriters had long called on MLB to integrate. By the 1930s, some white sportswriters joined the chorus. One such writer was Shirley Povich of the *Washington Post*.

> *There's a couple of million dollars worth of baseball talent on the loose, ready for the big leagues yet unsigned by any major league clubs. There are pitchers who would win 20 games this season for any big league club that offered them contracts, and there are outfielders who could hit .350. . . . Only one thing is keeping them out of the big leagues—the pigmentation of their skin. They happen to be colored. That's their crime in the eyes of big league club owners. . . . Just how a colored player would be detrimental to the game has never been fully explained.*
>
> Source: Shirley Povich. "This Morning With Shirley Povich." The Washington Post, April 7, 1939. ProQuest.

Landis died in 1944. Albert "Happy" Chandler took over as commissioner. He had a much different view about black players in baseball. Chandler pointed out that blacks had fought for the United States in World War II, which ended in 1945. They served and died for the country. Chandler and others believed they should also be able to play major league baseball.

Commissioner Albert "Happy" Chandler believed players of all colors should be able to play Major League Baseball.

It would take a special player to successfully break the color line. He would have to be talented enough to compete. Yet he would need to be tough enough to face the negative reactions. The Brooklyn Dodgers had just the right player in mind.

Brooklyn Dodgers president Branch Rickey set out to end baseball's color line.

CHAPTER 2

Rickey's "Great Experiment"

Baseball's color line had bothered Branch Rickey for a long time. By 1944, the Brooklyn Dodgers' president had quietly hatched a plan to end it.

An incident years earlier had influenced Rickey's thinking. He was a college baseball coach at the time. One night, his team stopped at a hotel. But the hotel manager told Rickey that one of his players could not stay there. That player was Charles Thomas. He was the team's only black player. Rickey was angry. He finally convinced the manager to let Thomas stay on a cot in Rickey's room. Rickey later saw Thomas rubbing his hands as if trying to peel the skin from them.

RED SOX TRYOUT

Other major league teams had toyed with the idea of signing black players. Jackie Robinson had a tryout with the Boston Red Sox in 1945. The team wanted to play games on Sundays. A Boston politician said the team could do so only if it offered tryouts to black players. Robinson was one of three blacks invited to a tryout. He hammered balls off Fenway Park's famous Green Monster in left field. He launched balls over it. But the team never signed Robinson. The Red Sox top scout reportedly said, "What a ballplayer! Too bad he's the wrong color."

"It's my hands. They're black," Thomas sobbed. "If only they were white, I'd be as good as anybody then, wouldn't I, Mr. Rickey? If only they were white."

"That scene haunted me for many years," Rickey later wrote.

As the Dodgers' president, Rickey's job was to field the best team possible. He had scouts who helped him evaluate players. In the 1940s, he sent his top scouts out to find the best black players around. Rickey hinted that he was looking for players for a Brooklyn Negro Leagues team. But the truth was he wanted to find a black player to join the Dodgers. This became known as Rickey's "great experiment."

The scouts set out to find the perfect player. If they picked the wrong person, the failure could set black players back for years. One name rose to the top of the list: Jack Roosevelt Robinson, known to most as Jackie Robinson.

Jackie Robinson was a multisport star in college.

Jackie Robinson was born in Georgia in 1919. His mother moved the family to California when Jackie was one. The Robinsons did not have much money. They had to bear insults from white neighbors.

On fields, though, things came easily for Robinson. He was a star in baseball, football, basketball, and track and field. When he tried tennis or golf, he was good in that, too. At school, kids would sometimes offer him lunch or treats if he would be on their team.

Robinson poses in his Kansas City Monarchs uniform during the 1945 season.

Robinson became a four-sport star at the University of
California, Los Angeles (UCLA). He later served in the US Army
during World War II. After Robinson left the army, he joined the

Kansas City Monarchs. They were one of the best teams in the Negro Leagues. Robinson quickly stood out as an all-star shortstop. Those Dodgers scouts noticed.

Rickey set up a meeting with Robinson in August 1945. Robinson thought it was about joining Rickey's Negro Leagues team. Not exactly.

"I've sent for you because I'm interested in you as a candidate for the Brooklyn National League club," Rickey told him. "I think you can play in the major leagues."

Robinson was stunned. As Robinson sat there, Rickey began pacing the room. Rickey needed to give Robinson an idea of what he might face. He screamed nasty insults at Robinson. Rickey threatened to kick him. Rickey pretended to punch him. For this to work, Rickey told Robinson, he would have to ignore it. All of it.

Rickey explained that all eyes would be on Robinson at all times. The player would face intense pressure and discrimination. But he could never lose his temper or start a fight. Doing so would give people a reason to say that blacks did not belong in baseball.

IN THE News

Robinson agreed to sign with the Dodgers after his meeting with Branch Rickey in August 1945. The *New York Times* reported the deal once it was made official two months later.

For the first time in the long history of organized baseball a Negro player has officially been taken into its ranks.

Branch Rickey, president and part owner of the Dodgers, yesterday announced that Jack Roosevelt Robinson, Georgia-born Negro, had been signed by Montreal of the International League, an organization in which Brooklyn owns a controlling interest. . . .

Signing of this player, according to Secretary Harold Parrott of the Dodgers, was not a sudden move to be interpreted merely as a gesture toward solution of a racial problem. Robinson was signed on his merits as a shortstop after he had been scouted for a long time.

Source: "Montreal Signs Negro Shortstop." New York Times, *October 24, 1945. ProQuest.*

Rickey was looking for a ballplayer who could excel in the major leagues. But he wasn't necessarily looking for the best black player.

"I'm looking for a ballplayer with guts enough not to fight back," Rickey said.

Robinson, *second from right*, signs his contract with the Brooklyn Dodgers on October 23, 1945. Dodgers executives look on.

Robinson convinced Rickey that he could be that player. Two months later, the Dodgers announced that they had signed Robinson. In 1946, he would play for the Montreal Royals. They were the Dodgers' top minor league team.

Rickey's "great experiment" was about to begin.

CHAPTER 3

"Well, This Is It"

Robinson was excited to report to spring training in 1946. But on the way from California to Florida, the plane made a stop. Robinson and his wife, Rachel, were told they needed to get off the plane. White passengers took the Robinsons' seats. Jackie and Rachel had to take a long bus ride instead. It was a sign of things to come.

Robinson finally arrived at spring training on March 4, 1946. Dodgers players and other minor league players were already on the field practicing. When they saw Robinson, they stopped and stared. Their eyes stared intensely at the black player. Robinson put on a uniform, turned to a team executive and said, "Well, this is it."

JOHN WRIGHT

Montreal actually had two black players in the spring of 1946. The Dodgers signed Robinson first. They added a black pitcher named John Wright soon after. He had been a star in the Negro Leagues. Many thought Wright might make the majors before Robinson. But Wright did not play well in spring training. Many people think the pressure and the taunting got to him. By May, he was sent to the lower minor leagues. The next year, he was back in the Negro Leagues. Wright never made the majors.

A couple of days later, a man came by the house where Robinson was staying. Robinson had not been allowed at the team hotel. The man said that Robinson had to be gone by nightfall. If not, the man said there would be trouble. Robinson quickly packed up and headed to Daytona Beach, Florida. Practice was set to resume there later.

Similar incidents followed throughout spring training. In one of his first games, Robinson smacked a single. He stole second base. Then a teammate had a base hit. Robinson raced around third and slid home . . . *SAFE*!

Waiting, though, were the police. They told Robinson he had to leave. In that town, it was against the law for blacks and whites to play on the same field.

Even Robinson's manager did not want him around. Montreal manager Clay Hopper was from Mississippi. The roots of segregation ran deep there. Hopper had begged Dodgers president Branch Rickey not to put Robinson on his team. But Rickey would not give in.

Robinson started slowly in spring training. But soon his skills took over. He began smacking the ball all over the place. He made tremendous plays in the field. He flashed his speed running the bases.

Finally, the Royals opened the regular season at Jersey City. Robinson stepped up to bat. A fastball came in. And a fastball went right back out. Robinson smacked a three-run home run over the left-field fence. He finished the game with a home run, three singles, two stolen bases, and four runs.

Robinson was well liked in Montreal. But he faced vicious insults in other cities. He remembered his conversation with Rickey, though. Robinson ignored insults. He let his glove, bat, and legs do his talking. Robinson hit a team-record .349. His 113 runs scored were the most in the league.

The Royals, meanwhile, had a great season. They won 100 games and the International League championship. But Robinson

IN THE News

The Royals played American Association champion Louisville in the Little World Series. Robinson wrote that the abuse he took in Louisville had been the worst he faced all year. Sam Lacy of the *Baltimore Afro-American* was there.

Continued booing and hurling of epithets, and two obvious spiking attempts, marked Kentucky's introduction to mixed organized baseball as the Montreal Royals and Louisville Colonels divided the first two games of the Little World Series. . . . The boos and epithets, of course, came from the lily-white stands surrounding home plate and the infield. . . .

The efforts to spike Robinson were made by [two players. One] drove in with spikes high but, fortunately, they merely grazed Robinson's knee and put him on guard for any future rough stuff.

Source: Sam Lacy. "Robinson Victim of Rebel Boos in Series." Baltimore Afro-American, October 5, 1946. ProQuest.

was the star attraction. Huge crowds came out to see him play. Montreal set an attendance record. The team's attendance on the road nearly tripled. However, the fans included both supporters and detractors of Robinson.

Robinson, *right*, crosses home plate after hitting a home run for the Montreal Royals in a 1946 game.

The season ended in the minor leagues' Little World Series. Montreal won that, too. Joyous Royals fans celebrated after the final game. They carried Robinson around on their shoulders as they sang and cheered.

Before he left the stadium, Robinson saw his manager. It was Hopper who had begged Rickey not to put Robinson on his team. Now Hopper reached out to shake Robinson's hand.

"You're a great ballplayer and a fine gentleman," Hopper said. "It's been wonderful having you on the team."

Fans were anxious to see whether Robinson would be promoted to the Brooklyn Dodgers for the 1947 season.

Will He Get the Call?

Fans and sportswriters took notice of Robinson's standout 1946 season. They began to wonder if Robinson would soon join the Dodgers. Branch Rickey would not commit.

"I assure you that Robinson will receive the fairest chance in the world to make the Dodgers," Rickey told reporters in January 1947.

That spring, Rickey scheduled a series of exhibition games between Robinson's Montreal Royals and the Dodgers. Before one of the games, Rickey pulled Robinson aside.

"I want you to run wild, to steal the pants off them, to be the most conspicuous player on the field," Rickey told him.

IN THE News

In the spring of 1947, Sam Lacy of the *Baltimore Afro-American* asked what everyone else was asking: Will Robinson make the major leagues?

Robinson's entrance into the big show depends very much on (1) his own ability to play at top form through the coming exhibition series with the parent club and (2) a definite slack in the performance of Ed Stanky, the Dodgers' holdover at the keystone sack [second base] from last year....

If Jackie is good enough to step into a starting berth with the Dodgers, I firmly believe Rickey and Leo Durocher will both go to bat for him. And I also believe the reactionaries on the squad, if any, will accept the challenge.

Source: Sam Lacy. "On-the-Scene Dope on Jackie's Chances With the Dodgers." Baltimore *Afro-American, March 15, 1947.* Print. 1–2.

Robinson delivered in a big way. He played in seven games against the Dodgers. Robinson hit .625. And once he reached base, he was a demon. As he took his lead off base, Robinson bounced on the balls of his feet and took stutter steps. It was almost as if he were taunting the pitcher. As soon as the pitch was thrown, Robinson took off. He stole seven bases in seven games.

Robinson, left, steals a base during a 1947 game.

But there were still two big problems. First, the Dodgers had established stars at second base and shortstop. Those were Robinson's best positions. Then one day a coach threw Robinson a first baseman's mitt. The message was simple: This could be your ticket to the major leagues.

WENDELL SMITH

Wendell Smith was one of the top black sportswriters of the 1940s. Smith had been an outstanding high school pitcher. But after throwing a playoff shutout, he was told by a scout that he could not be signed because he was black. From then on, Smith worked tirelessly to give black players a chance. He publicly criticized team owners and the commissioner for baseball's color barrier. He arranged for Robinson's tryout with the Boston Red Sox in 1945. He recommended Robinson to Branch Rickey. He was often Robinson's roommate and travel companion with the Dodgers. For his work on behalf of black players and his coverage of Jackie Robinson, Smith was honored by the Baseball Hall of Fame in 1994.

The other problem was more troubling. Many Dodgers players did not want Robinson on their team. They were not friendly to him. Some players from the South were not comfortable with the idea of a black teammate. Several signed a letter saying they would not play with him.

Leo Durocher was the Dodgers' manager. When he learned of this, he was furious. Durocher called a team meeting in the middle of the night.

"I don't care if the guy is yellow or black, or if he has stripes like a . . . zebra!" Durocher roared. "I'm the manager of this team, and I say he plays."

As spring training ended, the Dodgers and Royals headed to New York. They would play a couple more exhibition games. But

Robinson, *right*, shakes hands with Dodgers manager Leo Durocher following a March 1947 exhibition game.

Rickey had seen all he needed to see. As Robinson got ready to bat during an exhibition game, a Dodgers worker handed a short note to reporters in the press box. It read, "The Brooklyn Dodgers today purchased the contract of Jackie Roosevelt Robinson from the Montreal Royals. He will report immediately."

Robinson signs autographs for fans on April 10, 1947, five days before Opening Day.

CHAPTER 5

A Major Test

Opening Day for the Brooklyn Dodgers was April 15, 1947. Optimism was in the crisp spring air. The Dodgers were starting another season. But it was a season like no other.

In the top of the first inning, a black man in a snow-white, No. 42 Dodgers uniform ran out and took his spot at first base. MLB crowds tended to be mostly white. Black baseball fans more often followed the Negro League teams. But black fans by the thousands roared their approval on this day. Brooklyn's Ebbets Field had never seen a crowd like it.

Before the game, a couple of Robinson's teammates came over to wish him well. But most ignored him. Some still were not happy he was on the team.

IN THE News

Reporter Arthur Daley was on hand for Robinson's first major league game on April 15, 1947. He wrote about the scene for the *New York Times*.

> The debut of Jackie Robinson was quite uneventful. . . . The muscular Negro minds his own business and shrewdly makes no effort to push himself. He speaks quietly and intelligently when spoken to, and has already made quite a strong impression. . . .

> A veteran Dodger said of him, "Having Jackie on the team is still a little strange, just like anything else that's new. We just don't know how to act with him. But he'll be accepted in time. You can be sure of that. Other sports have had Negroes. Why not baseball? I'm for him if he can win games. That's the only test I ask." And that seems to be the general opinion.

Source: Arthur Daley. "Sports of the Times: Opening Day at Ebbets Field," New York Times, April 16, 1947. ProQuest.

Robinson stepped up to bat for the first time in the first inning. He was greeted by cheers. "C'mon, Jackie!" and "We're with you, boy!" Robinson grounded out to third base in his first at-bat. He later reached base on an error and scored a run. The Dodgers beat the Boston Braves, 5–3.

Robinson, *right*, poses in the dugout with Dodgers teammates, *from left*, Spider Jorgensen, Pee Wee Reese, and Eddie Stanky on Opening Day 1947.

Four days later, the Dodgers played the New York Giants. A record crowd of more than 52,000 showed up at the Polo Grounds to watch. Fans lined up for Robinson's autograph. In barber shops and on street corners, he was the talk of the town.

But there were many ugly moments ahead. The Dodgers hosted the Philadelphia Phillies just a week into the season. Robinson

Robinson reacts after being hit by a pitch against the Pittsburgh Pirates in a June 1947 game.

walked up to bat in the first inning. As he did, insults rained down on him from the Phillies dugout:

"Why don't you go back to the cotton field where you belong!"

"They're waiting for you in the jungles, black boy!"

And much worse.

PEE WEE REESE

Harold "Pee Wee" Reese was the Dodgers shortstop when Robinson joined the team in 1947. One day, Reese heard a string of insults being directed at Robinson. Reese slowly walked over and put his arm around Robinson. The jeering stopped. "I don't even remember what he said," Robinson later wrote. "It was the gesture of comradeship and support that counted." The scene has been memorialized in a statue at a minor league ballpark in Brooklyn.

Robinson was so angry. He wanted to go into the Phillies dugout and punch somebody. But then he remembered the words of Dodgers president Branch Rickey. *"I'm looking for a ballplayer with the guts enough not to fight back,"* Rickey had said. So Robinson did not react.

But his teammates did. Dodgers second baseman Eddie Stanky shouted back at the Phillies. Other teammates also stuck up for Robinson. For the first time, he felt he had the team's support.

Robinson needed it, too. Opposing pitchers threw at him often, and he'd been hit by the ball six times by the end of May. He had dodged many more pitches thrown at his head. Base runners tried to spike him. Opposing fans threw trash at him. Opposing players pointed bats at him and made machine-gun sounds. And hate mail poured in. Letter-writers threatened to kill him and his wife. When the team would arrive in a city, players would check in at

a luxury hotel. But Robinson would be often sent to a run-down, blacks-only motel. It was a hard, lonely existence. Hatred was a constant companion.

It was not always easy to focus on baseball. In late April, Robinson was in a slump. At its worst he was 0-for-23. Many people said the slump showed he was not good enough for the major leagues. But by mid-June, Robinson was hitting .300. He led the Dodgers to their first National League (NL) pennant. Robinson was named the Rookie of the Year.

For Robinson and blacks in baseball, 1947 was just the beginning.

Robinson, *right*, slaps hands with Dodgers teammate Pete Reiser after hitting a home run in an August 1947 game.

Robinson attempts to steal home during a 1949 game against the Chicago Cubs.

CHAPTER 6

Jackie Robinson's Legacy

A s a boy in the 1940s, Ed Charles walked under a hot spring sun toward the local ballpark in Florida. He went to see Jackie Robinson play spring training games for the Brooklyn Dodgers.

To Charles and other young black boys of that time, Robinson meant hope. For so long, so much had been off-limits to blacks. But now here was Robinson, a black man, playing with the best white players. Even better, Robinson could hit, throw, and catch as well as any of them.

In 1949, Robinson was the NL's Most Valuable Player (MVP). He led the league in batting (.342) and stolen bases (37). He drove in 124 runs. Plus he led the Dodgers to the World Series

IN THE News

Robinson joined the Brooklyn Dodgers in April 1947. That July, Larry Doby became the first black player in the AL. The *New York Times* ran a United Press report about Doby's signing.

Following Brooklyn's precedent-shattering example with Jackie Robinson, the Cleveland Indians announced today the signing of Negro infielder Larry Doby and predicted that "within 10 years Negro players will be in regular service with big league teams...."

With Robinson proving a success as a Brooklyn first baseman and as a gate attraction, President Bill Veeck of the Indians indicated that a wide-open scramble for Negro players was now under way.

Source: "Larry Doby, Ace Negro Infielder, Signs Contract with Cleveland." New York Times, July 4, 1947. ProQuest.

for the second time in three seasons. Robinson moved to second base in 1948. And he became one of the best second basemen in the game. Robinson was an All-Star every year from 1949 to 1954.

Robinson's success in the major leagues opened baseball's door to generations of black players. Charles was one of them. The boy who ran home from school to watch Robinson later played eight

The Cleveland Indians' Larry Doby, *right*, follows through on a swing during a July 1947 game. Doby followed Robinson by becoming the first black player in the AL.

seasons in the majors. But even with Robinson's success, racial integration in baseball came slowly.

The Dodgers remained the front-runners. So were the Cleveland Indians. They signed Larry Doby in July 1947. He became the first black player in the American League (AL). In 1948, Doby helped lead the Indians to the World Series title.

But other teams were much slower to sign black players. Several still did not have a black player a decade after Robinson played his first game with the Dodgers. Many teams had just one black player. Those black players faced many of the same hardships Robinson had faced. The Boston Red Sox were the last major league

STEALING HOME

The Dodgers played the New York Yankees in the 1955 World Series. In Game 1, Robinson danced off third base. As the pitcher went into his windup, Robinson broke for home. Yankees catcher Yogi Berra caught the pitch and tried to tag Robinson. But Robinson had slid across home plate safely. Stealing home was one of Robinson's trademark plays. It is hardly ever done anymore. Including that World Series play, Robinson stole home 20 times in his career.

team to sign a black player. Elijah "Pumpsie" Green debuted on July 21, 1959.

Robinson was an African American. But darker-skinned Latin American players were also kept out of organized baseball for more than 50 years. Baseball is wildly popular in countries such as Cuba and the Dominican Republic. Robinson's success paved the way for players from those countries to reach the major leagues as well. However, desegregation took longer in society. Laws to ban racial discrimination and segregation finally passed during the Civil Rights Movement of the 1950s and 1960s.

MLB today is a kaleidoscope of colors and cultures. One team's lineup might feature a dark-skinned pitcher from Cuba throwing to a catcher from Venezuela. A black first baseman from the United States might take a throw from a Dominican shortstop. Before

MLB players all wear No. 42 on April 15 to celebrate the anniversary of Robinson's major league debut.

Jackie Robinson broke the color barrier, none of those players would have been allowed in the major leagues.

"Jackie Robinson gave all of us—not only black athletes, but every black person in this country—a sense of our own strength," wrote Hall of Fame slugger Hank Aaron. He, too, played in the Negro Leagues before reaching the majors in 1954.

Branch Rickey sat down with Robinson in 1945. The Dodgers' president told Robinson he thought he was good enough to play in the major leagues. He never asked Robinson if he was ready to change the face of baseball forever. But through his skill, his resolve, and his courage, that is exactly what Robinson did.

TIMELINE

May 1, 1884
Moses Fleetwood Walker, a black catcher, plays for Toledo in what was then the major league American Association. He is widely viewed as the first black major leaguer.

1887
Led by Chicago White Stockings player-manager Cap Anson and others, baseball's color line is soon drawn. By 1900, there are no blacks in organized baseball.

January 31, 1919
Jackie Robinson is born in Georgia. His mother moves the family to California when Robinson is one.

1945
Robinson meets with Branch Rickey about joining the Brooklyn Dodgers organization on August 28. The deal is formally signed on October 23.

1946
Robinson hits .349, a team record, and leads the Montreal Royals to the International League championship.

April 15, 1947
Robinson makes his major league debut for the Dodgers. He plays first base and goes 0-for-3 but scores a run in a 5–3 Dodgers win.

July 5, 1947
Larry Doby becomes the first black player in the AL when he joins the Cleveland Indians.

1949
Robinson is named the NL's MVP. He leads the league in hitting (.342) and stolen bases (37).

July 21, 1959
The Boston Red Sox are the last major league team to integrate.

1962
Robinson is inducted into the Baseball Hall of Fame.

1997
Robinson's No. 42 is retired by all teams in MLB. The announcement is made on April 15, exactly 50 years after Robinson's first game with the Dodgers.

color barrier

An unwritten rule that prevented black players from being signed by MLB organizations.

commissioner

The person in charge of major league baseball.

conspicuous

Highly visible or standing out.

discrimination

Treating people differently based on prejudice.

dugout

The bench area at a baseball field where the players and coaches sit.

epithets

Offensive words used to insult someone.

exhibition

A game that does not count in any league standings.

integration

The act of unifying things that had been kept apart.

pennant

A flag. In baseball, it symbolizes a league title a team has won.

pigmentation

The natural color of one's skin.

precedent

An example that sets a standard for future occurrences.

scouts

People whose job is to evaluate possible new players for a team.

slump

A stretch of games in which a player plays poorly.

spike

To injure an opposing player by either stepping on him or sliding into him with the metal spikes of the cleats hitting the player.

FOR MORE INFORMATION

SELECTED BIBLIOGRAPHY

Eig, Jonathan. *Opening Day: The Story of Jackie Robinson's First Season*. New York: Simon & Schuster, 2007. Print.

Lamb, Chris. *Blackout: The Untold Story of Jackie Robinson's First Spring Training*. Lincoln, NE: University of Nebraska Press, 2004. Print.

Rampersad, Arnold. *Jackie Robinson*. New York: Ballantine Books, 1997. Print.

Robinson, Jackie. *I Never Had It Made*. New York: HarperCollins, 1995. Print.

Wukovits, John F. *Jackie Robinson and the Integration of Baseball*. Farmington Hills, MI: Thomson Gale, 2007. Print.

FURTHER READINGS

Herman, Gail. *Who Was Jackie Robinson?* Illus. John O'Brien. New York: Grosset & Dunlap, 2011. Print.

Pederson, Charles E. *Jackie Robinson: Baseball Great & Civil Rights Activist*. Edina, MN: Abdo Publishing Co., 2009. Print.

Robinson, Sharon. *Jackie Robinson: American Hero*. New York: Scholastic, 2013. Print.

Smolka, Bo. *The Negro Leagues' Integration Era*. Minneapolis, MN: Abdo Publishing Co., 2013. Print.

Smolka, Bo. *The Story of the Negro Leagues*. Minneapolis, MN: Abdo Publishing Co., 2013. Print.

WEBSITES

To learn more about the Greatest Events in Sports History, visit **booklinks.abdopublishing.com**. These links are routinely monitored and updated to provide the most current information available.

PLACES TO VISIT

MCU Park
1904 Surf Avenue
Brooklyn, NY 11224
(718) 372-5596
www.brooklyncyclones.com/mcupark/mcupark
Ebbets Field, home of the Brooklyn Dodgers, no longer exists. The minor league Brooklyn Cyclones play at MCU Park. The ballpark features a statue showing the famous scene when Pee Wee Reese showed his support for Jackie Robinson by putting his arm around him.

National Baseball Hall of Fame and Museum
25 Main Street
Cooperstown, NY 13326
(888) 425-5633
www.baseballhall.org
The Hall of Fame honors the best players in the game's history and includes many historical exhibits and artifacts. The Hall of Fame library has many of Wendell Smith's original articles about Jackie Robinson.

INDEX

ABOUT THE AUTHOR

Bo Smolka is a former sports copy editor at the *Baltimore Sun* and former sports information director at Bucknell University, his alma mater. He won several writing awards from the College Sports Information Directors of America, including the National Story of the Year. He lives in Baltimore, Maryland, with his wife and two children. When he's not writing about baseball, he can often be found coaching his son's baseball team. He has written several children's baseball books.